MW00723619

Yankee Broadcast Network

poems

John F. Buckley
& Martin Ott

Brooklyn Arts Press · New York

Yankee Broadcast Network
© 2014 John F. Buckley & Martin Ott

ISBN-13: 978-1-936767-33-5

Design by Joe Pan.

All Rights Reserved. No part of this publication may be reproduced by any means existing or to be developed in the future without written consent by the publisher.

Published in The United States of America by:
Brooklyn Arts Press
154 N 9th St #1
Brooklyn, NY 11249
WWW.BROOKLYNARTSPRESS.COM
info@BrooklynArtsPress.com

Distributed to the trade by Small Press Distribution / SPD
www.spdbooks.org

Library of Congress Cataloging-in-Publication Data

Buckley, John F., 1970-
   [Poems. Selections]
Yankee Broadcast Network / by John F. Buckley and Martin Ott.
      pages cm
   ISBN 978-1-936767-33-5 (pbk. : alk. paper)
   1. Poetry. I. Ott, Martin, 1966- II. Title.

PS3602.U26474A6 2014
811'.6--dc23

                                    2014019657

10 9 8 7 6 5 4 3 2 1
FIRST EDITION

Acknowledgements

Many of these poems first appeared, in one form or another, in the following journals:

Australian Book Review	"Doppeldanger"
The Baltimore Review	"What I Watched on My Summer Vacation"
Barrow Street	"Déjà TV"
Beecher's Magazine	"Ghazalgate"
Breakwater Review	"Skycast"
The Chaffey Review	"Television Through the Ages: A Smithsonian Walkthrough"
Crab Creek Review	"Repairman"
The Dos Passos Review	"TV Dinner Theater"
Euphemism	"Our Favorite Poems We Can't Watch"
	"Synopsis of *Lusts of Midgard*, America's Favorite Viking Soap Opera, Season 37, Episode 229"
Euphony	"Fireside Chat"
Glint	"Madame Leah Bears the Weight of the Zoonoosphere"
	"Nightmares of a Late-Night Talk Show Host"
Jenny	"The Re-Invention of Television"
Lunch Ticket	"*The B-Team*"
The Madison Review	"Inside the Box"
Natural Bridge	"David Lister Versus the Remote"
Owen Wister Review	"Coming Soon to the Disaster Channel!"
The Packingtown Review	"Late-December Holiday Special"
The Penmen Review	"Drift Away to *The Archipelago of Dreams*,"
	"*Real Housewives of Wayne County*"
Pennsylvania English	"Come Marvel at the Catasquaphonous Carnival of *Dick Clark's Rootin' Tootin New Year's Eve*"
Perceptions Literary Magazine	"Sunny Raines"
The Pinch	"The Newlywed Game"
Rabbit Ears: TV Poems	"The Newlywed Game"
Raleigh Review	"Moon Shot"
Redivider	"Final Season"
Reunion: The Dallas Review	"Commercials of the Apocalypse"
Rougarou	"Screens"
The Round	"Gauging the Invasion"
The Southampton Review	"Better Living Through Television"
	"*Burn'ded*"
Switchback	"The Mermaid Behind the Glass"
Wisconsin Review	"The Day Walter Cronkite Died"

TABLE OF CONTENTS

Yankee Broadcast Network

TV DINNER THEATER

Admission is free, for the most part. Families gather
haphazardly, hunched over nuked entrees and cheese
plates, truth told with eyes facing forward. During
an episode of *Baghdad Nurses*, a teenager bruised

by jock hands swears to his parents he will enlist
in the Marines or else go Semper Fi with a machine
pistol in his gym class, his father transfixed by boobs,
his mother by blood, his dog yawning on death's door.

Four towns over, the news that the pastor's daughter
has missed her last two periods is drowned out by
the soft slicing of Salisbury steaks and the susurrus
of the televised crowds at his alma mater's big game.

She excuses herself and goes to the bedroom, eyes
a closet rife with bent wire hangers and reaches in,
pulls out the portable set and finishes her hot cherry
cobbler alone, watching *Dan and Clementine Plus Nine.*

In a basement rumpus room, a cement mixer in a Barry
Sanders jersey wrestles his sons for the sausage pizza,
and tells his wife he's bet the mortgage on the Lions
covering the spread, while she gorges on the handyman

on *Cougar Country*, believing the rust on the underside
of her car spewing through slush is not unlike her own
chassis, which could use a good pounding from a fresh
pair of hands, perhaps one of her sons' meaty friends.

The Ukrainian's Bolivian girlfriend tranquilly mimics wet
celebrities in the synchronized-swimming contest, slowly
fanning the air with her arms as he mentions he's taking
them both to Kiev, away from the reach of Jose and Sergio,

since he can't find the package, the one that they paid him
to babysit. All of the yushka and ceviche in the world
can't save either one from sleeping with the fishes when
her brother-in-law's ravenous friends discover it's missing.

Rectangles glow in syncopation in the East Quad dorm,
then the bombs started dropping, and the numb students
could not pull themselves up from plastic chairs or text
about the red lights, smoke plumes, soldiers with gas

masks. On HD sets and cable-connected smartphones,
mouths masticate a United Nations of dishes, but no
words are left in any known language to explain how
the bombs taste in windpipes and bellies, in dayglow.

INSIDE THE BOX

The TV factory looks lonely on the slope
above the abandoned warehouses and dead
vegetation, unkempt lots with colored glass,
staked plastic bags waving like flags at half-
mast, tired worker dragging in for the early
shift, supervisors in short sleeves and ties.

Too hungover for stairs, can Rick hypnotize
anyone spying his slow ascent up the slope
of the handicapped ramp, nowhere near early
and guts roiling sour, his gray wet face dead
to the light and far from the loading dock, half
a day wasted, ruing last night's twelfth pint?

Coworkers snap pics of his crooked nose, glass
jaw saving him from a worse beating. Rick ties
one on, gets paid his dues, sleepwalks half
in the bag, his pain an assembly line, a slope
with no bottom. Now his boss has him dead
to rights, his forced retirement coming early.

There was a time he arrived at work early,
took extra shifts, his pride reflected in glass
monitor screens, before the years rounded
his lines, softened his belly, invisible ties
of time and tedium pinning him to the slope
of his life, his former spark dimmed by half.

It didn't help that the plant was now only at half
capacity cuz of China, and his bosses up too early,
glued to phones, his ex Dawn on a slippery slope
of face-y friends and fuckos he'd ground to glass
before the restraining order, plus the penalties
at work, with her on last shift, when all's dead.

What's a guy to do when his picture's dead?
The sound still works on the left but has half
the volume on the right. Would wearing ties
and staying dry make him better? It's too early
or too late to tell. Nobody gets a magic glass
to see life lived. Just a flat world on a slope.

TVs blare out like the dead; a factory closes early.
Self-handcuffed in plastic ties, Rick breaks the glass—
too late for a better half, he tumbles down the slope.

LATE-DECEMBER HOLIDAY SPECIAL

The documentary flies beneath Santa's naughty meter, a secret camera in Rudolph's
nose capturing his reindeer tickle fights and sleigh-bell excursion with travel agent
Silvia de la Milagro. She calls him a saint beneath the red-red glow and we see
many things shake like a bowl full of jelly. Mrs. Claus later plucks a strange errant

straw from a haunch, retrieves the footage, and uploads it to YouTube, before
returning to the orca pen to feed Booster and Boomer and Rumor and Rocket,
Quasar and Quantum and Crandall and Crockett, with the phosphorescent albino
Porfirio, Santa's sleigh-team for underwater trips to Atlantis, Lemuria, and Mu.

Elves make the toys, but gnomes do the outdoor work: hew the lumber, mine
and smelt the ore, catch and carve the narwhal meat for North Pole larders.
Santa busts their unionizing attempts, makes off-color jokes about ginger snaps,
keeps them locked outside so muddy gnome boots don't sully workshop tiles.

The succulent festal board is conjured in a mammoth Easy-Bake Oven by a kitchen
of yeti, lovers of icebox Yahtzee and Jello shots, shit-faced sauciers and sommeliers,
bereft of knives since the tragedy with the missing children in the basement potato
bin, guardians of the secret sauce in the hoof-shaped flask in Santa's other sack,

which he keeps hidden since his drinking drove his wife to her sister's house down
in Boca Raton, followed by marital counseling with Sneevle the studded snow goblin,
two hundred Turkish delights an hour, even with the saint's discount. Then came a DUI
in Dubai during the off-season, a uniformed sand-white genie writing a smoky ticket.

Was he slave driver or slave, demigod of charity or hedonism, lover or fighter?
He wakes one morning wedged between Prancer and Dancer, hands as raw
as the missing sunsets on top of the world, but he has yet to hit rock bottom,
the elixir of mistletoe wine drawing his gaze to the cosmos, to the flickering

stars over Bethlehem, over Mecca, over Lumbini, over Qufu, many dusty cradles.
He ponders the mystery of his workshop's quadruple-A rating, Standard & Poor's
only such blessing, a steady shining light in his financial portfolio. He weighs
the pros and cons of cashing it all in after centuries of altruism and penance,

the ransom of riches available on the black market for airborne reindeer, time-
slowing sleigh, and lithe-limbed elves who know how to wield candy canes.
The camera pans across the Northern Lights twinkling in blood-shot eyes,
and the audience awaits the next chapter, the unforgiving nature of giving.

DAVID LISTER VERSUS THE REMOTE

Ninety seconds to *Scarfinger*. Not on the end table. Not by the pile
of magazines. Not between cushions, under a couch, behind the throw
pillows. Ah. On top of the wall-mounted TV, perched like a finch.

How did it escape the armchair holster? David questioned friends once
and family, but they seemed uninterested. The universal remote
ended up in the freezer, in the bedroom naughty bag, at a gnome's

feet in the garden, gently flecked with mulch, tucked and besooted
in the chimney flue. Several weeks of dependable access and easy
couchside surfing passed before the next vanishing act, and the call

to his therapist, who asked if "remote" wasn't just a metaphor for life
falling into itself, an existential lollipop, the search for a clear signal.
"*The B-Team* won't just watch itself," David told his ex-mother-in-law

as they shared another cigarette afterwards. "Just leave the station on
YBN," she suggested as they posted "LOST—REMOTE: REWARD"
flyers around the neighborhood, giggling like negligent babysitters.

Then there was the phantom flipping of channels and the watching
of everything but the TV. So tired that he didn't notice the replacement
remote left behind his car tire. Snap. Crackle. If he cut off his own

hand, would it stalk the dreamtime at night, until it could clutch again
the wayward device on the astral plane? Who or what left the bloody
bread crumbs that led him to reclaim the real remote in a sad Nebraska

diner? The police said he stole it, but they were ignorant of his connection
to the great unknown, the grip in his hands almost sexual as he mailed
the remote to the Dalai Lama just before getting zapped and tagged

like a side of inferior beef, shocked legs twitching on the tile floor.
After posting bail, David disappeared: wandered, globetrotting, tracking
whispers: the remote had reached nirvana, the remote had staged coups

in recently renamed countries, the remote had developed an affinity
for Thai massage, masquerading as a calculator in a complicated
Ponzi scheme. David had already given up hope when they reunited

on the Patagonian landing strip, wrinkled duct tape and stainless-steel
pins holding each of them together. Here comes the fuselage lights.
Here comes the mother ship. Together they will channel a sequel.

THE DAY WALTER CRONKITE DIED

Suicide bombings at two swank hotels in Jakarta hurt at least fifty
and killed at least nine. A baby delivered in a Rio de Janeiro *favela*
was destined for heartbreak and glory. We worked on "Miami" and
"Pantsless," overwriting old files on the way to improving the poems.

A day of mourning continued with hurricane force winds in Norfolk,
while three soldiers were blindsided by rockets outside of Basra.
Then we saw model/actor/surfer Braden Bacha released from self-
imposed jail on *Big Brother.* Why do you never see the end coming?

Chavez celebrated Bolivia's birthday and promised Zelaya's return
to Honduras. Obama spoke out at the NAACP, calling for bootstraps,
while John botched a telephone interview, wrecking his chance to get
benefits during a summer with no work, just creditors' inquiries.

Martin was wandering through narrow Barcelona, his pidgin Catalan
drifting out into the ether, lost in a stadium filled with pill hawkers.
Bartenders replaced glasses with cups, the narrative now unspoken,
soothsayers shimmying in front of painted backdrops, blinking eye.

Pope Benedict slipped in his bath in his mountain chalet, breaking
the wrist on his chief benediction arm. Forty-nine rough Mafiosi
in Sicily went to jail. Father McCleary ran a free hand down the rear
of Wright's pants, tucking inside the tail of the junior's dress shirt.

Truth took a cigarette break, then a drive through the countryside.
People could not remember seeing the wreckage, or cameras
clicking like birds without worms. Do you remember hearing it?
That's the way it is sometimes. That's the only tale that matters.

MADAME LEAH BEARS THE WEIGHT OF THE ZOÖNOÖSPHERE

After the lights, the cameras, the actions, the takings
of phone calls, the emails and human tweets, one
thought persists, shines forth like a beacon from mind
to mind, Trinidadian auntie to white-pawed Persian: *Mittens,
stop your folly. Even if you catch it—unlikely—the zipping
red laser-dot will never love you. Turn your murderous
heart to mice and unwary birds.* A faint, resigned mental
meow replies to her psychic advice as she scans the alley
for more strays to guide. If only the humans understood
how much their companions yearned to choose two-legged
mates. On her late-night psychic show *Meow-Woof-Tweet-
Speak*, she projects her lithe animal spirit to her beasts
who desire to eat feces, hump, lick noses, scratch eyes.
Her father was like this. Once in the Devil's Woodyard
she convinced a clan of red howler monkeys to treat him
like a reluctant mate: *¡Que venganza!* There is, of course,
a cost for her talents, curse-side of the potency coin: nights
spent tangled in bedclothes, dreaming of wild menageries,
never to be alone with her thoughts, no matter how tightly
she wraps her head in kerchiefs the color of solitude,
and each meal vegetarian by necessity, just the scent
of goat curry evoking visions of final anxiety as knives
slit throats and silenced bleating. She drowns all her troubles
in Ting and Absolut Citron, afraid she might turn *Son of Sam*
or *Tarzan*, villainess or heroine, able to save the world
with a global earthquake warning system of canine intuition,
or create her own *Planet of the Apes* with a humanless Ark
after monkeys learn to type the greatest work of art and cat
cowboys herd the masses across dusty plains. She sometimes
pumps her legs in her sleep, chasing sticks and human femurs,

each morning scratching her hairless belly, saddened by a short
supply of nipples. But as the more philosophical hamsters
would sing, *Roun' roun' roun' go the creakity wheel, wit' de high
high high, wit' de low low low.* She enjoys pleasures along
with pains, privy to the piping joys of matchmade shrews,
the languid gratitude of sloths cured of eating disorders,
ambitious goat dreams of chevre sculptures, the peaceful
battle plans of the buffalo soldiers and their prairie-dog
quartermasters. Sometimes she envies Haitian voodoo
priestesses, ridden by only one loa at a time, and one-armed
zookeepers born in the Year of the Dragon. She fears the day
when her neighbors evolve past drunken shouts and rattling
walls, the thoughts of people a camel's straw and hog wallow
away, politicians' dreadful barks, and belly scratching done
within the human sphere of tall fences and metal collars.

REPAIRMAN

The television department in the Superstore
is like a lodge fireplace or preacher's pulpit,
drawing problems and their people to the lights

I keep. Diagonal inches pull them, pixilated
and spellbound, to the grunts and grimaces,
the heroic couplings and impossible quests.

I must tinker covertly, heal without taking
stock of the double coupons and upsells
that spell some dollars less or more. I lead

my guests to the La-Z-Boy. I hand out universal
remotes and listen to their diatribes so that
they will keep coming to me to mend cracked

monitors and lovers' fatigue, spotty reception
and familial rejection. Two thousand channels
of distraction flow like a river from my guiding

touch. Toshiba and I will never speak hurtfully.
In the break room, Manika talks to her hair
about the hidden dangers of the jewelry

counter, about the fear of being strangled by
angry necklaces fashioned by children in China.
I ply her attention with pudding and mention

opportunities for adopting Guangzhou orphans,
a shot at karmic recalibration. "Not all Funyuns
are sour," I state to the manic Sporting Goods

twins, Oscar and Dieter, after their impressive
match of invisible badminton failed to attract
prospective brides to the yoga accessories aisle.

They nod and ask if Sony Watchmen "are being
still übercool mit die hotties?" I don't know
the answer; my last date was ages ago, with

a Methodist Sunday-school teacher who used
me to set up her Wii Active and lure over some
of the younger crowd interested in a sweaty

rapture. I sometimes gather the gang after
hours to help me stack the television monitors
in a giant pyramid, a sacred shape that radiates

positive ions. We gather in a ring and recite
knock-knock jokes, plan the next joint Sunday
dinner, bathe in the many voices directed

at us by flickering faces of fictional families,
clues on how we as individuals might join together,
my people, my flock, my target demographic.

BETTER LIVING THROUGH TELEVISION

Olga tried to recreate the ascension
of the fourth Musketeer with lunch tray
shield and the Terrible Mop from Janitor

Bill, but Mr. Jaymes intercepted her,
relegating her to cleanup duty, and shushed her
when she sang "Jailhouse Rock" like

a righteous Blues Sister. So she quit, formed
a detective squad with Snuffles the rat
terrier and one-eared feline sleuth Cherry

Jubilee, but Mrs. Balakian did not seem
impressed with how Olga solved her first case,
that of the missing husband, with blown-up pics

of a strange lady and him testing tomatoes at Safeway.
Olga switched genres, ages, acted like a real
housewife until her faux fiancée ran off

with her lunch money, until nobody cared
'cause she'd become a tough pill to swallow
since Health Class. Beautiful Caitlyn Coe,

her arch nemesis, had concocted a love
potion, mixing the urine of pet mice with tears
produced on command, leading to an awkwardly

flirtatious principal as Olga complained about pigtail
pulls. Olga protected herself with a phalanx
of boys armed with sticks tipped with deadly

dog doo. It was just like those soldiers safeguarding
Inga, the baroness in that bloody Nazi war movie
Olga fell asleep watching with her Grandpa

last Saturday on TV-87's matinee. She vowed
to rally her forces, such as they were, for a top-
secret mission of mud pies and mayhem.

But Caitlyn ambushed! Brainwashed her mother
and infiltrated her headquarters with spies, dastardly
brothers bought off with candy. RC Cola waterboarding

ensued in the belly of Ol' Iron Claw, bathtub of horrors,
her own mother scrubbing her memories, fantasies,
toweling her dry and dreamless, to be planted

beneath sheets, kissed twice to keep the ninjas at bay,
humming to the lullaby of the living room TV,
those great adventures ahead in an endless tomorrow.

GHAZALGATE

The latest scandal unfurls in infidelity, infinite infidels on the news.
Why are we witnessing a plague of human cicadas on the news?

In the long-awaited interview, the celebrity deep-throats a lime Popsicle.
His limpid face and favorite dessert pass for hard-hitting news on the news.

How many times have we seen the tease of *Comet Hurtling Toward Earth*?
Next time it may well be *How I Survived the Rapture* on the news.

Some drones were retrofitted to fling pamphlets and Boston cream pies.
American protestors sometimes swat invisible insects on the news.

The model-athlete should not have gotten behind the wheel that night.
No chauffeur, no time machine, no way to hide his red river on the news.

What we don't know can't hurt us; we became invulnerable last Monday.
Our armor-plated eyeballs attack the anchor's stiffer haircut on the news.

Twenty-four-hour rotation, factoids spun like liquor-store hot dogs.
Some politicos see red, and take a bite, others green, and relish in the news.

We can't get enough of body parts: face slaps, talking heads, no underpants.
The lovelorn dictator leaks his overly produced sex tape on the news.

A parliament of pundits calls the latest poll figures "center-wing sabotage."
Hands across the aisle disembodied by venal verbal machetes on the news.

Our hand-held cams shake from superstorms, bikinis, binge drinking, gun bursts.
We shrink, and learn to cloak our first impulses, living on the news.

THE MERMAID BEHIND THE GLASS

The fall of Atlantis is all our faults.
I'm glued to news reports of spontaneous
gills, my own legs fusing, the earth
becoming a surface for history scrolls.

No one remembers to feed the fish.
We let them comingle and fight like scruffy
tritons, each missing scales, neglecting the pets
we purchased after reading *Tuna Whisperer*.

Lost surfers are occasionally caught
in nets made of plastic rings and bags,
and nothing stops the Sturgeon Surgeon
from attempting to save a life or two.

We are sluggish on coral couches, fins
rooted in pudgier flesh. Swimming only
to the fridge and back for fried krill puffs,
and blame our bulk on omega-3.

We have a sense of drowning now,
high-rise apartments brushing the sea
bottom, kelp in the penthouse, cauldron
of foresight on a drenched back burner.

COMING SOON
TO THE DISASTER CHANNEL!

Tornado Week features *The Traveling Travails*
of Tracy, a rag doll that flew from Tulsa to Tallahassee,
her left arm torn when it toppled a telephone pole
in Mobile, Alabama, the snapping of the pretty hem

on her tiny gingham dress sawing Baton Rouge oaks
into splinters. Will she and eight-year-old Stacy,
her newly homeless owner, ever be reunited?
Tune in Tuesday at 9 PM for a whirlwind adventure!

Don't miss our 24-hour *Quakathon*, featuring rock's
greatest acts in a tsunami of entertainment
guaranteed to make you shake all night long.
All proceeds will go toward the Society for Early

Earthquake Detection. With your SEED money,
you will get your name graffiti-ed onto a satellite
that will measure the displacement of heat above
Earth's faultlines and the braying of household pets.

The creators of *Wakka-Ding-Hoy!* and *Flabboviddies*
have devised another phantasmagorical show
for young children and stoned dormrats: *Kitty-
Puppy Apocalypse* celebrates a bold, candy-colored,

nuclear-war-ravaged landscape populated
by enormous radioactive baby animals, cuddly
monsters who attack the children of tomorrow
who fail to learn reading, math, and the value of sharing.

The latest in disaster reality mayhem booms
into your living room with *I Doom*: wedding

bloopers of shotgun weddings gone wrong,
priests kissing brides, judo throws into seven-

layer cakes, raining screams and shattered dreams
in scorched-earth matrimony. Then grab your cool
shades and tall umbrella drinks for *Sun Tan Nation*,
where inevitable global warming promises beach

days in Fargo in February, dark, irregular moles
tender to the touch, and golden preteen wrinkles.
Sizzling Saturdays continue with *The Showering
Inferno*, a game show of nozzles and napalm,
and *Post-Rapture Meteor Swarm!*, which tracks
clusters of heavenly debris as they rain fiery woe
on Las Vegas, on San Francisco, on Apple Junction,
Iowa, on all lairs and the unrepentant unsaved.

Gather your friends for an end-of-the-world romp
with our *Black Hole Rollers* marathon: terrestrial
teens travel through their darkest moments
and reappear as jaded adults, synapses firing

from an alternate universe with new memories
of innocence tossed aside in the bedrooms of friends'
parents, pinpricks in their vision that swarm, that sting,
that suckle inward. This is the channel you thought

only appeared on other people's cable listings.
But now, before hand hits remote, cataclysm
descends, and you realize your fears have
followers, disciples of begging and end.

THE B-TEAM

Their pilot Mulligan was only crazy for golf, practicing his swing whenever he could: on the tarmac, in the air, fleeing over the vast North Korean groundskeeper cells. Otherwise, plenty of rest and fluids made his world go round, granting the energy and mental acuity to tackle each day's tasks, like diversifying his retirement holdings.

Their conman "Hands" was an artist in the fluidity with which he communicated with his arms and fingers, mesmerizing men and women in security uniforms to give up their goods, which is how they obtained the ancient Dodge Ram, HQ for the group's epic, scandalous, and sometimes illegal adventures.

Their driver, strongman, and mathematician A. B. Abacus could bench four hundred pounds and recite pi to the thousandth digit, often simultaneously, when he wasn't busy filling out the team's expense reports. Forger of iron catchphrases, he inspired millions of boys to recite, "I offer my deepest sympathy to the intellectually benighted."

Their leader, John "Patton" Doe, ran an Army Navy surplus store and pawn emporium, which spawned many of their lesser adventures: long runs through the night to pick up howitzers for Tom Hanks, erectile dysfunction drugs and military grade glow sticks for the tweaker ravers on the boulevard. Clenching a peppermint stick in his teeth

and spouting, "I love it when a gambit reaches fruition," he organized the most raging underground chess tournament in the Southland, one marked by the rescue of an eighteenth-century antique ceramic set and the seizure of twenty kilograms of bootleg Adderall peddled by Geert Van Wafel, that evil Belgian grandmastermind.

That was nothing compared to the last job: the recovery of gold medallions, crafted for the KKK, and hidden in Masonic lodge bunkers across the US, with former East German athletes guarding not just the coins, but a super-soldier formula rumored to endow the user with the verve of a hundred teenage men. The B-Team dared not guzzle much because half of them were taking blood thinners, but enough sipping occurred for a great midnight cow-tipping escapade to coalesce, one which could have ended in tragedy, or worse, capture, if Mulligan's remote-control helicopter had not masterfully distracted both a shotgun-toting farmer and A.B., tonic-drunk, dancing with phantom

scarecrows that turned out to be Jack Mormons posing as corn-belt Amish outlaws. The closest scrape with death came on a fishing trip in Appalachia, though, when Hands was caught teaching a preacher's daughter to speak in tongues using a pair of supple rattlesnakes, the caterwauling from tent flaps an alarm for Patton, facing impossible

truths about aging and reaction time, coming a little too late, two punctures in an arm, as the prowling ministerial father sprang from the woods with consecrated water from a sulfurous hot spring, dousing all parties, the B-Team's leader fumbling for antivenin, razor blades, whiskey, Mulligan and A.B. out of earshot at the rushing river, three trout from the limit.

MOON SHOT

Everyone watches General Jim, hero to trillions, some of them women.
His Joint Lunar Defense Command shines full on our screens each
Mega-Moonday, right before bedtime. I make the three-finger vow

of the worthy yet few: to fight all enemies, lunar and extra-lunar.
I gather the neighborhood lunar league, using the attic for home
base, with a window to watch invaders and mind-controlled moms.

Spacemen must hold their breath, hence the stinky trunk challenge.
A leak in the roof has rotted the leather lid and the granny panties
inside. Membership has its privileges; membership has its costs.

Three kids fell, unable to seal their lungs from the mildewosphere
inside their temporary tomb. We receive our orders from the Ouija
Board and open far too much airplane glue to create the wormhole.

I am on the losing side of the catastrophic vote to allow "lunas"
into our boy haven, and not even the fiberglass hazing can halt
Stephanie and Christy's ascend through the ranks, their earning

construction-paper badges for hand-to-hand combat, for moon-
walking across the roof, for correctly identifying JLDC arch-
enemies: the Nazi Tigers of Titan, the Sharkbats of Neptune B,

the Ice Cave Ghosts of Mars that spooked Skylab into a falling
star. I tie a walkie-talkie to a balloon, and the satellite beams
the husky voice of General Jim to us, though the girls argue

it's the UPS man. And there he is, the notorious imposter, mud-
brown uniform a travesty of paramilitarism. Through the window,
tracking his truck, we wriggle into the crabapple tree, fitting

fruitbombs into slingshot rayguns with popsicle crosshair sights.
I aim and aim to impress, and even as I am distracted by giggles,
I slip toward the earth and launch supersour missiles, the freed

world whirling, tractor beam pulling me toward General Jim,
toward the elite squad on the moon itself, into a darkness filled
with the shouts of vanquished foes and heroic escape velocity.

SUNNY RAINES

The weathergirl always dressed spectacular for the day,
bare legs and shoulders glistening in front of the screen
where she pasted suns; smiling, sedate with cloudy hats,
smothered in gray. Her favorites were the lightning bolts

sproinging like italicized exclamation marks, eager to get
to work splitting oaks or striking an unlucky park ranger
for the thirteenth time (still not a record, but impressive).
She dated a guy that reminded her of them, an electrifying

district attorney who wrapped her in his overcoat, rain
or shine. She was a secret sugar fetishist who enjoyed torching
crème brûlée on his back while they sunbathed on his balcony
without a stitch. As a girl, she believed that she controlled

the wind, that she captained the cumulus banks overhead
with her gale-force whip cracks of will and wily grins,
lying on her back in the meadows, before the encroaching
subdivisions blocked the views, houses without weather

vanes. Now only the tornadoes on television called her name.
It was difficult to be the woman they called girl. One day she
ripped the heartland to shreds with winter mixes, employing
the same vigor she used to tear up her producers' backsides.

She left the office drenched, shivering, a once-moderate cold
front in a high pressure system turned supercell, a rage thrusting
broomstraw into phone poles. Then came a call—with a raise.
She changed outfits, reported disaster averted amid frowny-face skies.

BURN'DED

"Yo, yo, yo, y'all, welcome to the first episode
of *Burn'ded*. I'm your host, Hayden Smunchner,"

and so it begins, as the youthful host lays out
the situation: an attractive woman, a false friend,

some innocent bystanders and actors, all secretly
caught in the crosshairs of five hidden cameras.

Back from shopping, back to the Miata, opening
the trunk to find a bloodied "dead" man there,

just as the "cop" cars pull up. The studio audience
giggles. What a mess! Has she been burn'ded?

The "dead" actor opens his eyes, having been
told he was playing a kidnap victim, and proceeds

to cuff the woman with her own Louis Vuitton bag,
causing the false friend to confess the real game:

she was the girlfriend and agent of the "talentless"
hack who had discovered that he was cheating

and decided to out him in front of the audience
before firing him, to boot. Has he been burn'ded?

The "talentless" hack wipes away crocodile tears,
serves her the subpoena. He is the bad actor's

identical twin, a process server for the courts,
letting her know that she, her agency, and its seedy

investors, including Hayden Smunchner, Inc.,
are being sued for fraud and reckless endangerment

of numerous child actors, some young enough
to use unironically an inane term like "burn'ded."

The security guard was himself a former child
actor, who is afraid that if he stopped standing,

the ground-up Darvocet sprinkled in his corn puffs
would kill him. He also has the only "real" gun,

firing at each of the five cameras, time on the shooting
range well spent when planning his showbiz

revenge. He stares down the best boy, a middle-
aged Persian from Glendale, and loads one last

bullet in the chamber of his nickel-plated
Saturday night special: "Who wants to get

burn'ded?" Such is the signal for the federal agents
secreted among the "innocent bystanders" to move,

swarming the guard, seizing his revolver, the pills
nestled in one pocket, *The Catcher in the Rye*

crammed in the other, the death threats handwritten
on *Hello Kitty* stationery, promising to make

the studio audience pay for their part in this
escapade, for faceless complicity in postmodern

crimes, for blowtorching the hearts of romantics
like him with butane illusions, leaving them

burned, dead in all but name, this episode meant
for him alone, among an audience of inmates.

TELEVISION THROUGH THE AGES: A SMITHSONIAN WALKTHROUGH

(Press a Button for a Brief History of Each Exhibit)

Blind, Homer thought it a new radio, one with strange pauses, still enthralling enough to inspire him to fashion fan-fiction epics of Achilles, Odysseus, Paris, and the other figures from his favorite program, *Bronzed Band of Brothers*.

Without her rampant insomnia, Sappho might never have come across *Lusty Ladies* (Volumes 1 through 9) late at night on a forbidden movie channel, lending her the gimmick needed to crack her crushing writer's block.

Confucius was the first to suggest that television messed with our *ren* and *yi*, and his actual quote was: "Before you embark to watch TV with your enemies, first dig two graves for the potatoes you become."

They sing of skinny arms and the poet, Virgil, who, exiled from natural buffness by genetics, scrupulously copied every exercise demonstrated onscreen by the young Iaccus Lalanneus, crying "*Aeneid* a hot *puellam!*"

The lost first biography, *Beowulf* in London, was created after the scribe monk who followed the hero on his early carousing years stumbled upon a flat screen projecting *Jerusalem Shore* in the Roman sewer aqueducts.

Alfonso XI of Castile chewed his darkened nails during the Battle of Gibraltar, watching the first hospital drama, *Black's Anatomy*, to howl at the other poor souls suffering bubonic plague and the sexy interns seducing the bloodletters.

Obviously, Geoffrey Chaucer learned words like *fart*, *interrogation*, and *slumber* from watching reruns of *Barnabas the Miller*, beloved sitcom of the mid-1370s, in which the learned Dietrich sowed new words among the sheriffs of Greenwich.

The visions of Joan of Arc came to her from a pirated signal that beamed the time-traveling adventures of fellow teens Ted and Bill, plutocrats of the Atom Age who battled parents, aristocracy, and degenerative brain disease.

In researching their respective renditions of the Faust legend, both Marlowe and Goethe nearly went broke giving their money to the fiery televangelists of *God's Very Cross*, which broke records by running from 1579 to 1826.

Surrounded by cameramen, the sound crew, and brioche-bearing production assistants, Marie Antoinette was in such a tizzy shooting her reality show *La Vie Simple*, that she neglected to keep each episode's budget in line.

Secretly unmoved by child labor and starvation, Charles Dickens wrote *Oliver Twist* upon discovering orphans in workhouses only had access to beadle-controlled basic cable, watched on antique B&W sets caulked with oakum.

Bram Stoker was an original *Twilight Zone* fan, watching the frightened sun wither every evening in the reflection of his unplugged TV that haunted his writing table, peering for signs of intelligence in the fading red streaks.

World War One would have utterly crushed the spirit of Ernest Hemingway had he been unable to interrupt the horrors of trench warfare with sunny daily episodes of *Live with Regis and Dawn* streaming in the ambulance.

It took only a few episodes of *Animal Kingdom Come* for a young Ayn Rand to pursue survival of the fittest with an almost religious fervor, spitting on Bolsheviks and riding Nietzsche like a broken saddle mount.

Einstein's hair ranked as his third most important discovery, inspired by the unkempt runner-up on the bootleg reality series *Barbery Coast*, where each loser had a close shave with their victor's sling blade.

Thank you for joining us! Please deposit your special glasses in the bins at the end of the corridor. Please return to your home pixel quadrants. Your accounts have been debited. Please wave goodbye as the lights dim.

REAL HOUSEWIVES OF WAYNE COUNTY

The drama started at Eva's reception held at Uncle
Jerry's mattress store. The police report missed

the bullet hole in the duvet but recorded Megan's
plan to stow all the empties in her Fiesta for the dime

deposits and the groom's drunken lap dance that led
to the half-assed Jägermeister Molotov cocktail

in the shower stall at the Packard Motel. And Jackie
really has to ask why Shauna won't lend Heather

her black mini skirt for her date with that hunk Karl,
who cruises Hamtramck in his murdered-out Ford?

If Eva and Jackie weren't cousins, their bumpers
wouldn't have locked during the parking lot donuts,

or idle the combustion of well drinks at Paycheck's
Lounge. No one knows who lipsticked the bullseye

on the Abdullahs' garage door, who left the half-
eaten bag of Better Made barbecue chips at the scene,

who started the candle wax fills at Dibbz 'N' Dabbz
nail salon. Relationships were chipped like the black

ice on Woodward, Heather and Megan tagteaming
Shauna, the *pączki* of sisterhood grown stale,

handheld cameras intent on capturing childhood
friendships made monstrous in snow and fading light.

COME MARVEL AT THE CATASQUAPHONOUS CARNIVAL OF *DICK CLARK'S ROOTIN'-TOOTIN' NEW YEAR'S EVE*

Dick was nervous: he never expected to live long enough to see
1884, much less be the man ushering it in on New Year's Eve.

But surrounded by production assistants in rawhide, clapped in
coonskin caps and clamoring for his babyfaced attention, he steadied

his nerves. Spectators' questions poured in: was he really the love child
of Meriwether Lewis? Would the crowd pouring into Longacre

Square from the Brooklyn Bridge, slugging back Routin and rum,
tear commuters' carriages apart? Why did Josiah H. L. Tuck ride

the first submarine like a bull? Did the Yankee Broadcast Network
telegraph operators, dot-dashing the fresh, iron-hot dance steps

of teenaged street urchins to stations countrywide, realize they were
ruining the country? Dick smiled, cracked his whip and sold tickets,

two cents for standing, four for a seat by the midnight inferno.
A Wild Bill Hickok impersonator snatched a megaphone prototype

from Thomas Edison, easing himself into a Vin Mariani bender,
and stirred up the crowd, which included H. G. Wells, staring skyward

at what appeared to be a helium balloon in the shape of a cartoon Eloi,
all limpid eyes and potbelly. High in its basket, social-media correspondent

Nellie Bly scanned the crowd for potential trendsetters, launching
a series of tweeting canaries to carry her messages groundward.

She wrote that Henry W. Seely was plugged in, electric iron
at the ready, shirt collar wings looking as though he might fly.

(More than one corset was tossed his way as midnight arrived.)
Sparks and flames reflected in a transcendent rack of teeth as

Dick ascended the bandstand, stepped to the light of the aerial
bonfire, ready to be lowered at the count of twelve. Folks held

their breaths, a zeppelin blinking to the rhythm of horseless riders,
as Nikola Tesla took in his first light show in the Big Apple.

The fireworks, broadcast in windows, reflecting a signal
that the future wanted to billow beyond the fenced frontiers.

OUR FAVORITE PROGRAMS WE CAN'T WATCH

Mom hates *Devastator Island*'s cool gore, and pops
us when we pretend to be Captain Carnage at church.

"Professor X is a gimp," Freddy taunts, undermining
my idol on the day I try to melt his Pokemon cards

with heat vision, not Dad's Marlboro lighter
like that doofus school rent-a-cop claims.

We search the girls' locker room for signs
of alien transformation like we learn from *Mitsu*

Star, the bootleg anime stashed in our bedrooms
on random weeks. Like terrorist cells on *America's*

Most Hunted, our Koran is *Urotsukidōji: Legend
of the Overfiend*, and we bow down to memories

of its probing limbs in the bathroom. Uncle Kenny
says when drunk that he and Dad had to survive

with diagonal boobies on the encrypted adult channel.
Grandpa swears the rotating channel listings contain

cryptic messages of the Rapture every seventh viewing,
but we distract him with virile cowboys and sad wives

on the Mexican soaps, and he screams for bullets
like he did in 'Nam. QVC sometimes sells us rabbit

vibrators when we sneak down for midnight grub,
and we worry about the fate of animals in small cages.

One network showed an edited Cheech & Chong movie.
We didn't get it, but our old, forbidden babysitter said

they're real funny. We learn to scan neighbors' windows,
department store TVs, and phone screens for the terrible

and tasty. Our own show is being filmed right now, caught
by shaking lenses, our wide eyes a lethargic alien armada.

GAUGING THE INVASION

Alerted by deep-space transmissions, the High Council of D%nev'Hra6b,
a sublime cloud comprised of the keenest minds from fifty-seven races

coalesced to consider the matter of an alien world, an orb filled with
the patter of Earthlings: primate, parrot, and porpoisoid. It was difficult

to discern the difference between mating cries and battle moans, a baby's
teething and jagged cliffs jutting from the land, the terrors of flatulent frat

boys and bomb-strapped terrorists, the many languages from monitors
melding into a bouillabaisse of sights, sounds, signals. Of everything,

only the GEICO Gecko, whose form is a Galactic Constant, proved familiar
and worthy. All else seemed chaos, the dust of a galloping seven-limbed

larvae churning in the nave of a temple. Nothing was structured, nothing
was strong, nothing suggested knowing the Thwuj Symbiotic Hypothesis.

The mystics and mathematicians could not understand the lost years,
the cavemen and eyeball money, deviations from the ur-quest to race,

belch flames, and seed the sky with poisonous smoke. This desire
toward devolution and a future of lifeless machines lay rusting in ditches

rather than hewing vatgrown flesh in glorious gladiatorial clashes sent
chills down the triple spines of the winged-martyrs manning the scanner

arrays, willing to suffer and shrive for hopeful transmissions of carnage
and sacrifice. What kind of monsters make Dexter stifle his red thirst?

Why must the Borg lose? Why did that beautiful, angry genie thwart
Major Nelson's mission to turn the moon into a mecho-magic breeder

colony? Night sweats invade the worried dreams of the Sleestaks as
Chaka toys with Holly's braids. Over and over the waves from Terra

crash against the receivers. Were the twisted transmissions themselves
the weapon, a kaleidoscopic psy-ops barrage of karmic contusion and

anthropochauvinist screeching? An ovoid Clatterworp slid from his post
in agony, staring into space and weeping *Guy Fieri, Guy Fieri, Guy Fieri!*

The invasion ended without a sunspot cannon, or magnetic poles realigning,
but fifty-seven races deciding that endless derivations of hero quests

and unintended mating rites, vast empires losing interest in all but themselves,
ignoring the bulk of an enthralling cosmos, were best left to languish alone.

DÉJÀ TV

Though we witness it, we mistrust the rapture:
a man races to the airport to stop his lover,
those events predestined to undress the curtains,
the sister that kisses her brother on the lips.

A man races to the airport to stop his lover,
his cab driver filled with slow-speed malice.
The sister that kisses her brother on the lips
draws the short straw to disarm the dirty bomb.

His cab driver filled with slow-speed malice,
the weary cop with six hours left before retirement
draws the short straw to disarm the dirty bomb;
the criminal half-sibling takes the fatal bullet.

The weary cop with six hours left before retirement
drives the car off the bridge and into the river.
The criminal half-sibling takes the fatal bullet.
An ex-lover, breaking from her hostage bonds,

drives the car off the bridge and into the river
to drown the symbiotic alien life form.
An ex-lover, breaking from her hostage bonds,
is no longer the hero with the secret identity.

To drown the symbiotic alien life form
we must learn the true subject of the prophecy
is no longer the hero with the secret identity,
an end-of-the-world declaration of love.

We must learn the true subject of the prophecy,
those events predestined to undress the curtains.
An end-of-the-world declaration of love—
though we witness it, we mistrust the rapture.

SKYCAST

Hear the clamor from Mount Olympus
echo through the cloudless blue sky,
no thunder, no Titanic resurgence,
just the howling of Ares, who is missing
the USC-UCLA game because Aphrodite
won't stop watching *Glamourella*.

Whenever the remote control is missing,
the pissed-off pantheon blames Hermes.
Zeus flicks bolts to station hop with such
poor results that Dionysus points out beer
models that perhaps need his static touch.

Before Hestia left, she and Demeter
could agree on cooking shows,
but Zeus and Hera's desires almost
never coincide, just on principle, nor
do they snuggle during the Olympics,
which suffer from a lack of real drama:

The follies of poison and wobbly legs,
the ripping of limbs from fallen foes,
the kidnapping of athletes' families
to make them race faster than the four
winds, to jump higher than the golden
chariot slicing the sky into bloody orbs.

Apollo himself tends to refrain from
the kvetching about who gets to pick,
but marvel, ye mortals, at his radiant
pouting when twin Artemis records over
sweet *Delphi City Limits* on the DVR
with *Cypress Sally's Buck Hunt* marathons.

Everyone hates when Poseidon visits.
It's all about undersea documentaries
and cartoons where he's depicted in
a starfish crown, the latter enough
for Athena to question his ambitions.
Eventually the TV turns to wrestling—

on both sides of the screen—plastic
cups of ambrosia spilled on the sofa,
Ares distributing noogies to sisters,
Phoebus handing out solar wedgies,
until mighty Hercules picks up the set
to smash it over Hades' dark head.

The pieces end up in the rumpus room
next to a bent harp and an Olympia Beer
sign on the fritz, with Hephaestus forced
to rebuild the cosmic set with 4D tech,
his swollen feet a sad testament to how binge
watching *Lost* episodes humbled a smithy god.

NIGHTMARES OF A LATE-NIGHT TALK SHOW HOST

Sometimes, during naps, the others mugged him in his dressing room—
Leno and Letterman holding him down while Conan and Craig stripped
his pockets, grabbing every linty wad of market share. Nobody heard
him whimper, nobody saw him writhe. It was like that time in Chicago.

He'd left his Budweiser on the bar, and the local radio jock spiked
his drink with some wicked nostrum, and he woke up naked on the L.
His fear of broadcasting nude during his stand-up monologue made
him check daily to see if the cameras added ten pounds *down there*.

Some nights he came to in a sweat, haunted by the pieces his stalwart
Judas bandleader played, cloying classics he had only once confessed
he still loved guiltily, mightily. In these dreams, the audience jeered
at his open weeping to Climax's "Precious and Few," among others.

He could not forget Camille and the way he used to place a phantom
microphone beneath her lips, until she confessed her infatuation
with a sexy TV star, and the realization that it had never been him.
Her side of the bed was a twisted knot, unfit for guests to interview.

Lunestra, Ambien, each pill a loaf of bread, a staff of life threshing his
consciousness, leaving him pummeled beneath thousand-thread-count
sheets. But even the pills could not beat back the images, fever plays,
operas on wrestling grandmothers, his producer's schadenfreude arias.

His tongue swelled to the size of a small rodent, and he lanced it to make
room for his opening monologue. Blood dripping was rarely funny,
but this flowed down the front of his shirt, out the studio doors, and
into the street, as his laughing sidekick deftly kayaked the ruddy cascade.

He feared dandruff, undersea earthquakes. He feared giant moths that writhed
beneath his shoulder pads. He knew his set was really just the front-window
display of a secondhand-puppet emporium, a tableau of polished wooden jaws
and limp heartstrings, and here again comes Geppetto to hoist him back home.

SYNOPSIS OF *LUSTS OF MIDGARD*, AMERICA'S FAVORITE VIKING SOAP OPERA, SEASON 37, EPISODE 229

Bleikr apprentices himself to a wandering
skald, despite his parents Abjörn and Gunna's
wishes that he become a pillager of towns,
or at least hamlets. Abjörn must pay thirty
bags of gold to the shadowy Vigmarr or lose

his dragon-prowed longboat. Vigmarr discovers
that father and son Hálmi and Haurr are the mighty
sisters Hálma and Haurlaug. The League of Hacked-
Off Legends, relegated to guzzle battles and barmaid
wrestling, start a riot in the great dining hall when

their sons return to croon of conquests of waves,
war, and women. Ivar the Boneless jolts the Jutes
with a jelly-kneed genuflection, a sign of sincere
fealty to them and a foul betrayal of his lord
and liege Lidsvaldr. Could the cold-hearted caresses

of Kolfrosta, vile village vixen, have led him astray?
Kolfrosta leaves to fetch more mead for the men
but goes missing anon. Ingvar Iron Eyes bolts his war
helmet to his oversized head and butts every root
and melon to pulp to protest his son Rollo the Rancid,

local hero for perfecting pumpkin mead and carrot
soup, unworthy pursuits for the heir of a liege
that has ravaged his liver and Normandy. Haurlaug,
her heroic identity no longer hidden, actively hews
a troll in half with the axe of Hákr, the valiant

yet vulnerable Valkyrie vying to capture the heart
of Thórgils, whose thundering throng has brought
back a bevy of attractive Waterford crystal tableware
from the monasteries of Ireland. Bothilda the Buxom
madly pursues her love affair with a dragon father

who burrowed into her dreams to ask her to torch
all of the vessels in the harbor. Will she succumb
to the numb breath that fogs her breast plate,
or refashion her shield into a basket to hold
her unborn child, the myth, the saga to come?

FINAL SEASON

Grandpa taught me to spell, guest starring on *Almond Avenue*
as The Silent E, turning *cap* into *cape*, *twin* into *twine*. I watched
him live on both sides of the screen, the one on the couch older,
more tired, but more likely to give out candy, a wrinkled piñata.

He told me the first number of any day was always number one,
then certain numerological derivations of the creative force divined
from the *I Ching*. Then had me carry those numbers to his bookie.
It was a practice picked up in Singapore after his tour in the Marines.

After his third bout in the hospital, when I was old enough to sit
in the waiting room by myself, watching him strut across the screen
in reruns of *The Green Thorn*, rugged mid-Seventies eco-avenger,
he moved in with us for good, Mom's latest dying houseplant.

The neighbors grew used to him running around the garden
in his flowery underwear, offering to help the birds, dogs,
and cats by composting their feces. When his agent called
for the "role of a lifetime," my mother eagerly drove him

to the boat show at the mall near Castaic Lake, an audience
of commuter cops and their families fretting to see the man who
had played Officer Lawson, Colonel Rick "Popcorn" McPhee,
Sheriff Ned, and other uniformed stand-ins for absentee dads,

like my own canceled rerun of a father. Mom and I watched him
proudly as he nailed his lines before forgetting his name. That night
he fleeced me with the shell game he felt should be perfected
by any hustler or actor. *To be the ball*, he said, *was to be a man.*

COMMERCIALS OF THE APOCALYPSE

When even the walls began to turn on each other
and kids kicked around skulls in the wreckage for fun,
from skin to sin they sought to sell us things, and so
advertising was born again. Who can forget Zom-B-Gone

with its blend of seventy-three special herbs and
pesticides, able to repel hordes of undead salesmen
and make scorched lawns lush once more? Doesn't
everyone still hum the jingle from Crazy Ed's Eyeglass

Emporium and the double-eye-patched pirate's *ayayays*?
The almost-banned Snuggie Tug Blanket was the most
asked-for item many an irradiated winter, the half-smiles
of the bundled boy in the ad used as a flirtation device

at many a mutant's ski lodge. *The new Ice Age was
never so cozy*, both heads cried. And hundreds of
urban hunters took part in the Chef Boyarmegeddee
Recipe Sweepstakes, in which no meats were off-limit.

Everyone loved the colorful death threats on the promos
for *Dancing with the Scars*, where losing face happened
every show and the limbo costs more than just fingers
and toes. And who can forget the all-purpose Gunsu,

love child of pistol and Swiss army knife, slicing
a can in half at twenty paces, extracting a stranger's
kidney for resale at thirty? *But wait! There's more!*
Every child safely tucked in the Emerald Zone wanted

the Donner Decoder, a fat tester for tweens in the Crimson
Zone to meal plan when helpless toddlers and old folk
got separated from the pack. The infomercial zoomed-in
on a posse herding kids to where the grass is always redder.

But the very best commercials originate once a year
on Thunderdome Thursday, when clashes between
champion motodeath mavens and cyberdoom aces ring
out across the airwaves, punctuated by ads for such

necessities as spear-proof undies and spike repellant.
The crowd cheers for the next round, the latest toys,
free of the ambition that clouded the world and set it
all aglow. Never is there yearning for the good old days.

WHAT I WATCHED ON MY SUMMER VACATION

Mom said she can't afford a sitter since they took Mrs. Sanderson away.
And all my toys are stupid since I turned eight and a half. And I'm not
allowed to cook on the stove since the smoke from the cheese fire killed
the fish. So I eat peanut-butter sandwiches and watch a lot of TV.

Sometimes my friends come over to join us on strange adventures,
our couch a fully battle-ready assault vehicle in case things get weird,
as they sometimes do when Uncle Leo makes us scoot over to bet on
baseball, smelling like the floor of Mom's car, and almost as sticky.

We go to the village picked on by Zombiezilla, Iguana From the Grave,
who bit the head off that one guy and made the island ladies scream,
who made everyone huddle indoors until the team of uniformed scientists
came with their giant robot and punched the undead lizard into hot magma,

which flows across our living-room floor, trapping us on the couch.
Jimbo, our sister's boyfriend, smokes funny cigarettes that give him
the power to walk on lava fields and fly high above the giant ants
he swears marched from the TV, alien spawn, above the teenage kids

in spandex representing the rainbow and kung fu power punches. We
soon form our own gang, needing safety in numbers, especially after
the black-and-white bandits broke free from the hoosegow and rampaged
through the den, smashing the vase that came all the way from Taiwan.

We fight over whether we would eat the dog or cat if the peanut butter
sandwiches stop raining down onto the stinky-belch island of Dad's
hairy belly, the worst picnic table ever. The ninjas on the screen
encourage us to chop off one another's heads with paper-plate Frisbees.

Sometimes, orphaned kids step out from the flickering shapes and Mom does not look up from finishing her sudokus to notice that she is yelling at parentless newsies with leg braces to stop singing, set down their yellow journalism bundles and wee hobo bindles, and eat some porridge.

In the kitchen, the remaining lights of summer flicker beneath tinfoil-covered antennas, and we grow milk mustaches and worry about losing our eyes to September, a picture of classrooms with tiny stick figures at desks, each drawing an exit route lost in the long days behind us.

DRIFT AWAY TO
THE ARCHIPELAGO OF DREAMS

Coming this fall on YBN...Welcome to *The Archipelago of Dreams*,
an island paradise accessible only by sleepgliders drifting off course

to where you'd truly rather be. Here you'll find Mr. McApnea, and his
giant sidekick slug—don't be afraid—Pierce, who'll mewl, "The Portal,

The Portal," when guests slide into this cross-dimensional limbo, guests
like the Cookie Mamacita, the diminutive heartstruck songwriter,

who brandishes the limbo stick for each perilous snoozeland adventurer.
Slip beneath the pole, beneath the threshold, slip feet first into one

of a million fire pits, crucibles where your deepest regrets turn to ash,
to topsoil, and from which springs a smarter, more beautiful version

of you, but deadlier, a doppelgänger who will chase you across the moss
fields and mushroom hilltops, into the fiberglass cloud topiary garden,

where pink cumulus elk bushes rear near your duo of faces, itchy slivers
wafting down into your hair (like a buoyant soufflé bouffant baked by

the Ministry of Insouciant Cheer), but the hair helmet and lederhosen
are no great disguise in this halcyon harbor. You ask yourself who you are,

carbon copy, mass hysteria in human form, a lover's Bruce Banner,
a soldier's Don Juan, a spoiled barracuda wrapped in an army blanket,

returning after these special messages ring like a tinfoil molar alarm.
The commercials snap you back into the family room, rubbing

your eyes and staring at the macramé owl on the wall, at Frito bits
ground into the shag carpet—a life lived on tiny islands of sofa cushions.

You are the land bridge from the panoply of secrets beneath throw pillows
to the test pattern that buzzes, to a sun that exists or doesn't behind curtains.

FIRESIDE CHAT

The fireplace has been replaced by a TV
cracked open like a dinosaur egg, a blue
flame flickering inside the screen. President

Smunchner, half-ruined face still swoonworthy
from the right, patiently waits for the drums
to subside, for children to trust they won't be

eaten. The purple mountains proudly wear
their scars, a length of battlefields smoking
onscreen like Tinseltown toughs. His voice

is low, clear, reasonable—there'll be extra
rations for rebuilders. His words are not
important; they rarely are. He has taken

the country as a bride, the smoldering
dream of courtship denied. Vows billow
out from a mist drifting across the studio.

One of the teary cameramen won't stop
whispering, *History Is Just a Country Road,
Take Me Home.* The President scarcely

pauses as Secret Servants whisk the crying
man away for tea and reconditioning.
He adjusts his patch, scans the tiny screens

of hopeful eyes reflecting his performance
upside down in irises, searching for some
way to liberate the actor falling to earth.

DOPPELDANGER

Scoring forty-nine flesh wounds in sixty-five episodes, federal agent Mark Sterling
and Soviet superspy Vladimir Volkov faced off in five seasons of *Checkmate!*,
cheeky Cold War television thriller, two foes united in mutual personal respect
and marrow-deep loathing for the ideals of the other. Who could have known

the lights would never go out, the syndication deal triggered, the fan sites
pulling them into cutting repartee and verbal barbs that led tabloids to cover
the shooting of the film version from pre-production to post, the vodka contests
leading to juggling extras and sharing the co-star of the film on three-way dates?

Marco Crespi wanted his Sterling to be much less stalwartly Yankee, more liberal
and tortured, able to join in on civil-rights marches without smelling subversion.
Franklin Willingham Randolph, IV, the man behind Volkov, sent millions to
John Birch and Goldwater, felt his ice-blue eyes smolder at every damned hippie,

every war left unfunded. Their famous poster of two men posing on chessboards
among shattered pieces had graced not only the walls of *Contemporary Art Magazine*
but was also lampooned in late-night skits. Still, their graying temples insured white
would always take the first turn in battle, and the off-Broadway musical *Checkmates*

brought in hip-hop and the seeds of Afghanistan, something beyond their mid-Sixties
swagger and cigarette impunity. No Emmys, no Oscars, just twin eyeblink cameos in
the inevitable ironic reboot, with those sprats Hayden Smunchner and Jeff Philip Sousa.
Residuals went into funds for mutual ex-wives and rival urologists, who prescribed

each loads of pain meds for hematuria, blood murky as the ideological river of urine
seeping between them, their death bouts not dissimilar from ballroom dancing
when played and replayed in slow motion. When depressed, they call each another
and change places, reverse accents, deny transgressions, defy their stale brotherly selves.

THE NEWLYWED GAME

He loves that she loves karaoke, that she sings karaoke—
or that she sang karaoke, that she loved karaoke before

they stopped going out because she didn't want to miss
Yankee Yodeler. Now they can play special marital games

in the living room, with the blinds drawn. They wear
a week's wardrobe and strip every time the Italian supermodel

on *Design Drama* waves *ciao!* In a ring of couch pillows,
they mock-wrestle, giggle and tickle in time with the Federal

Fighting Federation announcers' shouts, until the dreaded sleeper
hold of post-coitus arrives, and the victor trolls for fresh partners

online. She picks the opposite sports team of his to cheer for,
winner dons the handcuffs, special leather items in the locked

table drawer. She remembers how he carried her to bed on his back
like a child, when she got drunk, instead of tying her up

for his webcam; a time when clemencies meant more than Tuscan
monthiversary dinners, him shaking her father's limp hand.

The truest pleasantries remain unspoken. Now they watch *Apartment
Invaders* for clues on vanquishing nations, one room at a time.

They sometimes wake to ghostly images after infomercials
and before-chatter of the day's weather, the dead space

between programs forming dust bunnies in their throats.
Hooting for the competitive eaters on *The Craw* has grown

passé. Work has drained them, and dinner is another episode
of *Judge Jackie*, plaintiffs reminding them first of relatives,

then themselves. They often forget where they parked
the car. Their cat has migrated to the dryer with chew toys

and kibble. He hates that they both depend on the late night
psychic, the one that warned them of love, the one who

laughed too long while congratulating them with news
that the reality show they were living was renewed.

SCREENS

The first TV consoles squatted like solitary,
heavy ankylosaurids on living room carpets.

Then came the domestic herd, flocking to kitchens
of mothers whipping new recipes, to bedrooms

for itchy children with chickenpox, to dads'
dens for the game. The radios were stashed

away, and we lived in the shadows until color
arrived, articulating ethnicities, the surround

sound tickling our necks like pesky poltergeists
on a bender. Next came the Super Bowl parties,

glass bowls of salsa, antennae and submarine
sandwiches, a tiny step to the portable monitors,

handheld, pocket-sized, on wristbands, on
necklaces, on ceilings in dentists' offices.

Lovers placed them in belly buttons to make
their labors easier, not nearly as dangerous

as the streaming steering column or rifle-
mounted satellite dish during deer season.

Henhouses swooned to a silky stillness when
farmers mounted flatscreens on coop walls,

each chicken laying eggs while agog at all
carnal exploits of foxy soap-opera villainesses.

Who can deny the power of HD streaming
in the church confessional booth, rigged

pacemakers set to broadcast *Space Ghost*
for vascular surgeons? But those watchers

are pikers compared to those souls glued
to a looping *Twilight Zone* marathon inside

cracked Katrina-ed crypts across the Mississippi
Delta. Everywhere, we see screens and screens

see us, filter and watch us become us, our window
nannies, blessed panoptical prison cathedrals.

THE RE-INVENTION OF TELEVISION

One-point-seven million years ago.
A savanna on the outskirts of another
savanna. Three anonymous hominids
combine sheets of shale, vines, the juice
from primordial berries, lightning bugs,
and the circuit board from their tribal
GPS, which happened to be the spine
of their departed medicine woman, one
with unerring direction. The first rabbit
ears were a form of hare ancestor without
the hops. Everything was fueled by fire:
flame shadows crackling its mnemonic
static, laugh tracks recorded in the hearts
of coals, red-lit shadow-puppet commercials
projected platonic on the smooth cavern wall,
applause signs inscribed in smoke. Reality
shows sizzled within the steaks of mammals,
whose sturdy femurs were featured in home-
improvement programs. Tar pits syndicated
the comedic moments of men hauling ass
from fanged terrors, each vertebrae projecting
passions like pixels on a bleak screen.
The Pleistocene Department of Standards
& Practices cut out two-thirds of all mating
hoots on the Homo habilis telenovelas,
but that couldn't stop a new breed
from syndicating their dramas and follies,
from inventing religion as a novel way
to sell more stones, from sending new
actors into battlefields and bedrooms,
from jumping the last surviving shark.

ABOUT THE POETS

MARTIN OTT lives in Los Angeles, where he writes often about his misunderstood city. He is the author of three books of poetry: *Underdays* (Notre Dame University Press, 2015), *Captive* (C&R Press), and *Poets' Guide to America*, co-authored with John F. Buckley (Brooklyn Arts Press). In 2013, he published the novel *The Interrogator's Notebook* (Story Merchant Books). He blogs at writeliving.wordpress.com.

A recent graduate of the Helen Zell Writers' Program at the University of Michigan, JOHN F. BUCKLEY has been writing poetry since an attempt at writing a self-help book went somewhat awry. After a twenty-year stint on and near the West Coast, he now lives in Ann Arbor, Michigan with his wife. His website is johnfrancisbuckley.wordpress.com.

MORE LITERARY TITLES
FROM THE BROOKLYN ARTS PRESS CATALOGUE

All books are available at www.BrooklynArtsPress.com

Anselm Berrigan & Jonathan Allen, *LOADING*

Alejandro Ventura, *Puerto Rico*

Bill Rasmovicz, *Idiopaths*

Broc Rossell, *Unpublished Poems*

Carol Guess, *Darling Endangered*

Chris O Cook, *To Lose & to Pretend*

Christopher Hennessy, *Love-In-Idleness*

Dominique Townsend, *The Weather & Our Tempers*

Jackie Clark, *Aphoria*

Jared Harel, *The Body Double*

Jay Besemer, *Telephone*

Joanna Penn Cooper, *The Itinerant Girl's Guide to Self-Hypnosis*

Joe Fletcher, *Already It Is Dusk*

Joe Pan, *Autobiomythography & Gallery*

John Buckley & Martin Ott, *Poets' Guide to America*

Joseph P Wood, *Broken Cage*

Julia Cohen, *Collateral Light*

Lauren Russell, *Dream-Clung, Gone*

Laurie Filipelli, *Elseplace*

Martin Rock, *Dear Mark*

Matt Shears, *10,000 Wallpapers*

Michelle Gil-Montero, *Attached Houses*

31758790R00044

Made in the USA
Charleston, SC
28 July 2014